T0066900

Aries Vs. Aries

To: All of my Aries sisters
All colors all shades
And all women all over the world.
Check this out

WANDA REYNOLDS

Order this book online at www.trafford.com
or email orders@trafford.com

Most Trafford titles are also available at major online book retailers.

© Copyright 2013 Wanda Reynolds.
All rights reserved. No part of this publication may be reproduced, stored in a
retrieval system, or transmitted, in any form or by any means, electronic, mechanical,
photocopying, recording, or otherwise, without the written prior permission of the author.

Printed in the United States of America.

ISBN: 978-1-4907-0852-2 (sc)
ISBN: 978-1-4907-0851-5 (e)

Trafford rev. 07/26/2013

 www.trafford.com

North America & international
toll-free: 1 888 232 4444 (USA & Canada)
fax: 812 355 4082

*H*ello: My name is Wanda D. Reynolds. And I was born and raised in New York City, I live in the Bronx all my life. My mother raised me and my mother met my father Richard C. Reynolds. My mother was 18 years old. My father rest in peace Dad. He was 24 years old. My mother had 3 children with my father, but both have passed on rest in peace li'l bro li'l sis. But before my mother met my father she was in another relationship and had a son which was my older brother, he passed on rest in peace big bro. Now my mother had 4 kids, 2 girls and 2 boys, now I'm the only one left. My father was a slick sneaky dope fiend. But check this, my dad was a fuckin' fly dopefiend in the 70's when dope was for two dollars a bag and my father was 6'4". He wore a size 14 shoe. My father had to get his clothes tailor made. The only shoes my pops wore were Stacy Adam Shoe. My pops would perm his hair to keep his hair permed with finger waves. Like Leon from the Temptations and Robert Townsend from the five heartbeat. When my pops didn't have money for his dope my pops would pawn his stacy adam shoes to the pawnshop when he need his dope. My pops would rob and stole from my mother. I remember I used to see him beat my mother. My mother had black eyes quiet often. My mother fought back believe me she is a Capricorn. But I still love my father, I remember me and my siblings were watching the Brady Bunch my mother was at one of her friends in the building, my mother was on the second floor. I lived on the 3rd everytime he came in high, him and my mother would fight. He took my brother his son rest in peace P.Nut no not P.Nut it's my brother David which pass on also rest in peace. My father who is not David's father took my brother David and put his right hand in scolding hot water. He took his daughter rest in peace little sis. He took and threw my sister against my mother highfi, put a mark on her eye that she took to the grave with her. My sister died April 16th. I didn't find out until June me and my family. Jacobi hospital didn't try to contact my mother at all. Me and my sister and brother P.Nut are Aries. Me and my sister were born 4-12-63 and 4-12-55 P 4-16-64. She passed away on P.Nut birthday 4-16-2012. My family didn't find out until 6-17-2012 my sister had a close casket. My sister died 4-16-2012 and was born 4-12-1966. Anyway getting back to my father, after he did that he told me to go get my mother from down her friend's house as we were coming upstairs I was crying, I told her what happen. She came in the apartment, my father slapped my mother and when he slapped my mother they were fighting in the kitchen and my mother grabbed a knife and stabbed my father 1 inch from his heart. My mother was in a very abusive relationship. My mother almost went to jail for that. But those were the 70's try that shit now and see what happens. Fuck around and get football numbers. I remember my father punched my mother in the eye, my mother couldn't work for a week. So back in the 70's it was a gang called The Black Pearls. My mother's brother in law was the leader. I remember my mother calling her brother in law and his spouse to attack my father and it was done. That how much she hated him she got them to beat my father with a heavy chain. The chain was like real heavy like chains they used to lock up vacant property my father was curled up in the hallway crying. I couldn't believe what I was seeing my mother telling me to get back in the house. I was crying I will never forget that as long as I live. Then after her and my father split she met another man. My father and mother broke up when I was 5 years old. Then she met another man. He raised me from 5 years to the age I am now, God rest his soul. So after my pops split and went to jail and short after then came my step father who took me as his daughter me and my siblings. He was a good man I guess cause he was a drugdealer. But to me he was abusive to my mother also. They fought, my mother always worked all her life. Until she got custody of my 2 sons who were 3 and 7 years old at the time. That is another chapter I remember he sold dope out my mother apartment. They went on vacations a lot. My Aunts and Uncle would babysit. I remember the cops kicked my mother door down with a ram looking for drugs. It was like 6:30 am so my step father took and threw the drugs down the toilet and flushed. But as soon as the fucking door came down here go the police asking me do I know where the gun is. I said I know, I knew where the gun was, he threw it out the 5th floor back yard windows. They had dective all the basement looking for a gun in a pile of garbage. I don't know whether they found it or not. Well anyway my mother went to the women pentition Center for 18 days. The 42nd precinct locked them up. Her man did a few years mom would go visit him on visiting day, never missed a visit. And did state time, now all probably wondering why I'm telling you all this O.K well I was in a very abusive relationship since 1984 until 2012. It all ended when that bastard went to jail. Now I met Raihem in 1984. We lived in the same building, we live in 184 Street Grand Ave. He lived on the first floor, I lived on the 2nd floor, now mind you I was going on 17 years old and he was also 17 years old. But we didn't see each other again until I was 21 years old. His birthday is 4-7-63, mine is 4-12-63, but when we met again I already had a 5 month old son, and then came along Raihem son who is now 26 years old. Raihem is also a grandfather, he has a beautiful 7 year old granddaughter. She's my first grand baby and if you are out there Eyliyah D. Reynolds me and your father are still looking for you. Grandma been trying to find you Eyliyah for 5 years. The last time I seen my grand baby she was 2 years old, now she is 7 years old. God do not like ugly what goes around come around. I hope and pray I see Eyliyah D. Reynolds.

She has 3cousins in Fayetteville NC. Who would like to see her. I got four beautiful grand daughters Tyliyah 7 years, Heavenly 7 yrs, Honesty 4 yrs, and Harmony 2 years old. Now Tyliyah need to know her cousins like I said God do not like ugly. Anyway getting back to Raihem when we got together at 21 years old, I fell in love with him to say I never thought I would see him again. Anyway one day I was on my way to my mother house pushing my son in his carriage. He was only 5 months old, my sister was with me, we were walking down Jerome Ave. 161 st. Yankee Stadium to get the D. train to go to my mother's house who lived on 183rd street. I used to work at the Stadium in the 80's. Anyway me and my sister looked at each other and said there goes Raihem, my sister never liked Raihem. If he really wanna know and I'm talking to him. MY sister rushing me to get the D. Train Uptown, anyway he asked me where I was going I said to my mother house for a little while. So he asked for my phone number, so I gave it to him. So he said can he stop by later on. I said it won't be a good time cause I was still dealing with my son's father. But eventually we broke up. When me and my son's father split my son was 2 years old. Rest in peace baby. Anyway then along came Raihem. But if I would have left Raihem in the street and never let him in my life, maybe I would be mean to him so mean to other men who tried to talk to me. All the anger and pain, hate I have for Raihem now. I'm not gonna say I hate Raihem I take that back you don't suppose to hate that is a strong word like love is a strong word. So I don't hate Raihem. I don't like Raiherm, and

I'm not inlove with Raihem no more. Anyway when I took Raihem into me and my son's life I really thought he love me. But he didn't, he used and abused me since 1984 until 2012. The 3rd day in my apartment on 705 Gerard Ave. Apt 21-G at around 9:00am I got up took me a shower it was a nice summer morning. When I got out the shower I got dressed ate. What I always eat in the morning back in 64 was Apple Jacks Cereal Tap. Raihem told him I be back in like an hour I was going to Thom McCan to buy me another Dr. Pennie Pat Leather Loafers. I had them in Blk. Patent Leather. I was going to buy them in red. So the best and was acting like he was sleep. Cause when I came back to my apartment the door was open. Raihem was gone and so was my 13inch brand new color tv and my black zip off sleeve blk. Leather Michael Jackson jacket with the silver buttons and padded shoulder. Rest in Peace Michael Jackson. Anyway I felt like a real dummy. And before he robbed me, we had sex cause it sure wasn't love, so after tv and jacket episode. I was tight, I knew Raihem liked hanging out in Disco Fever on 167 street that were he met all his hogs at. Anyway when I did catch up with that bastard was 2 weeks later. I felt like a fool. Anyway he lived on Fullton Ave. 169 street across from the Health Department. So I know he had to ride the 55 bus to get to Fulton Ave. He used to hang down town in Harlem on 125th street, 123rd street, 119 street. He was a professional pickpocket, this niger been picking pockets since he was 12 years old. And he is 49 years. He lost his touch cause if he didn't lose his touch he would not be up state doing a pick pocketing bid now. I'll said it again God do not like ugly. I repeat God do not like ugly. So when I did catch up with Raihem it was around 10pm waiting for the 55 bus. He didn't see me I crept up on that mother fucker this is before the bus pulled in the bus stop. Raihem thought he seen a ghost. He started talking all fast sturring. I said I don't wanna hear it, just replace what you took you have a week if not I'm pressing charges on you. I don't care how you get it just get my 13inch color tv and my jacket back, so he went out and hustled up my money. Raihem was a professional pick pocket. He's been pick pockets since the 80's and 90's. He got caught on 86 Street in Midtown Manhattan in 99 and Did 3 years. And I was a booster I started boosting in the 80's also. I stopped boosting 99. When Raihem went and did that 3 yr. bid up north Raihem had been going to jail since 21 years old. That when I had his son I took his son to Otisville Correctional Facility Raihem did time in Clinton Correctional Facility Sing. Sing Correctional Facility Downstate Correctional this mother fucker been in almost every jail up state. I went to jail for Raihem while I was 3 months pregnant cause him my brother in law got in a fight in my living room in the 80's. Raihem sold my brother in law shirt. He stole from Florshiemon 125 street the shirt was a red white and black leather shirt. Remember the 5 heart beats when they first met their manager and they were practicing dance steps at their manager house. Now I remember it was a red double knit with black and white leather in the front with red button. Raihem sold him the shirt for

$50.00. But at the time my brother in law only had $ 25.00 so Raihem agreed with that until Friday he would have gave him the other $25.00. Raihem could not wait until Friday so he comes in around 2:00pm in the afternoon all cracked up talking about the wants his shirt back to me. First of all I told him y'all made a deal Raihem was not trying to hear that shit. So the crack head goes in the living room wall now the shit is on. Now mind you Raihem was all cracked out Raihem didn't really want nothing so me and my dumbass goes in my kitchen comes out with a broken machcet. Swug it to my brother inlaw's right arm. When awk ass Raihem back up remind you I'm 3 months pregnant. My brother inlaw had to get stitches. I went to the cops I did it. I figure I'll get out cause I'm pregnant. Well the judge wasn't trying to hear it. I went to Rikers Island for the first time for 7 days. Now the state was going to take over. But my brother in law drop the charges God is good all the time. Anyway while I did the seven days Raihem brought this skunk scassy wag to my apartment. Fuck this shoe for 7 days on my living room floor. He bought the bitch from Disco Fever on 167 street. Talking about she had no where to go. When they put the cuffs on me outside the building he yelled from the window I lived in the on the 6th floor in the front. I should have took my keys from him. Anyway when I got out after 7 days my sister were waiting for me outside the courthouse on 161st. So when I got outside my sister and her man was telling me sorry I wasn't trying to talk to them cause I was still mad for my sister pressing charges on me. If she would not have press charges Raihem would have not have bought that bitch in my house. Anyway him and my sister started running down the block to Gerard Ave. I lived right down the block from the precint. The precint inside 161st yankee stadium they got there before me. They knocked on my door. I was hiding on the side they knocked Raihem yelled who is it. My sister said me. He would not open the door talking about Wanda is still in jail. That when I told them to go down in front of the building then I knocked on the door. He said Wanda's not here. I said Oh yeah mother fucker I'm here. Now mind you when I put my keys in the door the door suppose to open right well I locked it. The faget was fucking that stickin bitch with my door open. Any when I got in all I seen was some bitch going out my living room window just bra-panties. When my sister and her man seen her my sister rest her soul snatch the bitch from the first fire escape, the bitch went running down river ave. in Broad daylight. With just her funky bra set on. The bitch had an overnight bag I threw that bitch shit out the window I threw his funky crack head dust head herion head out of my house. He was scared to go downstairs cause my brother in law wanted to whip his ass. Raihem was scared. So when he got downstairs. Raihem ran like the bitch he is. A couple of days later I found out I had V.D Raihem said I gave it to him. So he rushing me to Lincoln Hospital to get a shot in my ass. He said he never cheated on me. O really so you are saying I gave you V.D. Raihem. Yeah how I got it I said you stinking fucky crack head. Raihem got raped on Riker's Island when he was 16 yers.old. Cause Raihem got the Puerto Rican hair looks like a Doimoin stand 6'3" tall. That faget stayed in the mirror more than me. When we were in our teens me and Raihem lived in the same building. When we were 16 he lived there before me. I could have been with him at 16 yrs.old. But we bump into each other on River Ave. When we were 21 years old. Raihem spit food in my face twice over the years. He threw bag of my food out the window in 2002. When he got out of jail one day I washed Raihem clothes. So he get up one morning took a shower. I didn't see Raihem for 3 days. When I seen Raihem again he did not have no boxers on. But he left 3 days ago he had on boxer. He claim he never wore any out the house so that proves right there you are a dog. One night me an Raihem been up all night getting high. So the next morning I got up wash my face and brushed my teeth went in the kitchen to fix us some breakfast. Which was homefries with onions and green peppers, scrambled eggs bacon and toast. And some coffee that's how good I treated the ungrateful dopefiend. He didn't appreciate what I did for him. So he must have smelled the bacon coming from the kitchen cause he had called me from the bedroom and I went to see what he wanted. He asked what I was doing I said I'm making you breakfast in bed. He said know put his breakfast to the side, so I said I won't cook your home fries yet. When you are ready to eat them I will fry your home fries. Anyway check this, after I fixed my breakfast. I came in the bedroom sat on my side of bed. Turn on my cable now the bastard is saying where's my breakfast bitch. I said you just said you will eat later. So I said you gonna have to wait a few minutes for the potatoes. In the meantime I'm scrambling him 2 eggs and putting 4 slices of bacon in the oven. It cooks faster to me then I put two slices of toast in the toaster. Raihem likes black coffee folgers to be exact. So he rushing and calling me all kinds of names. Next thing I know he getting dress so I got kind of nervous. So I started walking from the bedroom. Next thing I knew was an iron coming at me full force. I'm glad I turned around to watch him. And got away from the flying iron. If that iron would have hit the back of my back he could of mess up my spine or something. Then he goes out and slam the door. I was glad when that punk leaved. I hurry and locked my door told him I hope he gets busted and go to jail. Cause all he did was go to midtown and pick women's pocket books. Raihem been picking pockets for years. So here he comes 4 hours later he rings the bell so I took my time going to the intercom. So about time I got to the door he was ringing the doorbell when I open the door he didn't say shit just went to the bedroom got his ash pipe pulled out his crack cocaine his two bags of herion and two pks of new ports. Now mind you I'm still in the living room watching my cable while he got me cable on the bedroom. Mind you he was paying my cable bill. I was on welfare getting 46.00 every two weeks 200.00 a month in food stamps. So mind you remember before I said I use to boost well I had to while I was on PA. I would go boosting every Saturdays down 28th street. When they sold all the bootlegs name brand pockets. Boots leg name brand clothes those people that was selling all that take name brand couldn't really call the cops. If they catch you stealing cause if they get caught the cops is gonna take it also so shit I miles well get some. I was making 300.00 to 400.00 everytime I hit the 28th street. When he was picking pockets he wasn't helping me pay my bills If I made more than him. He had to hustle to pay my bills boosting for me was like a job. A 9:00 to 5:00 lots of days when my cable bill was due are my con-ed. I had to go to hustle up that bill money. Lots of days I didn't like going shoplifting. But I had no choice cause I damn sure wasn't going to sell ass. So I had to do what I had to do. But later on God bless me with SSI. It's nothing to brag about but it's better than 46.00 every 2 weeks. Raihem would make his money by picking pockets. And would go elsewhere for 3 and 4 days at a time. Come back smelling like a funk box. And I don't suppose to ask him where he's been. You ain't laying your stinkin ass in my bed. You should have wash your ass where you was at. Now you wanna come dirty up my bathroom. I met Raihem like I said when he was 16 years old that is around the time he got raped on Riker's Island. That's when he started getting a taste of being behind bars. But to me Riker's Island is a play pen. Wait until he hit state grounds. Now that prison any way Raihem came back into me and his 26 yrs. Old son's life in 2002 from Clinton Correctional and is still on the same case. And it is now 2012. And mind you he is in jail right now. He suppose to get released 9-25-2011 from a correctional facility up state. Mind you I'm in a women's shelter right now in Brooklyn, NY. Now he knows I'm homeless so parole is going to ask Raihem where will he go. Believe me if I was to bump into Raihem the first thing would come out of his mouth is that he is in a men shelter. Everything comes out of his mouth is a lie. You know where Raihem is going when he get out of jail. With one of his crack dope fiend girls. But he said he's at a shelter. I really don't give a fuck where he goes when he get out. Cause that creep ain't going to last six months. I said Raihem stop having sex with me in 2008 everytime he came home doing 90 days he would promise me sex. Talking about after he take a nap that faget would come up with all kinds of excuses that okay he don't know what he got good until it is all gone. I've been used and abused by this man since the 80's up until 2012. Now I been to all his upstate bids never missed a visit. I went to Clinton Correctional Facility. And it was a lot of snow up in Canada. But I bet you I was there he was surprise that I came. And a lot of times when I would come see him he would always get restless around 2:00pm. He would ask me to leave talking about he don't wanna get caught in the count. I mean too me he didn't respect my visit. Lots of days it be could in the mountains. He didn't care as long as he can get what he wants. I remember one time Raihem had did a couple of months on Riker's Island when it was almost time for him to get released he told me when he getting out he suppose to had came to me on a Friday guess when I see Raihem Sunday evening. You know what

I did. I mess around. I ran into one of my exes I invited him to my house Sunday afternoon for Sunday dinner I used to always cook my Sunday dinners. You name it I can cook it. I can bake cakes real good and pies even banana pudding. So I get a knock at the door. I said who is it he said Raihem. I asked him what he wanted I told him to come next Friday. Cause I'm busy so now he banging on the door all crazy. I said threw the door you got released Friday niger today is Sunday. Talking about he was hanging with his boys for 2 days yeah right. Bitches was there too I guess he thought I had dummy on my forehead. So when I did open the door my friend was sitting in my living room on my rug. I was sitting on my living room set I paid for while on welfare. I layed away 600.00 living room set he was hating he didn't say it looks nice Raihem was always jealous of me cause I'm a strong Aries, and he is a weak one. One day we didn't have no food in the house Raihem knew that. That before ACS took my boy in the 1988 cause of Raihem. I was getting my check and food stamps the next day. All I had for my sons to eat was a box quakers oat meal 1 pound box sugar half stick margarine, that welfare rice and welfare beans you get from the PJ. You gonna stand online and get the PA food anyway that's all I had ACS knocked at my 10:30 pm. If 1988 talking about they found my 7 years old riding the downtown Dtrain. He wound up in Coney Island last stop on the Dtrain. This man white seen my 7 yrs. Old son sleeping on the train. He woke my son up and asked him was he lost he said yeah. God was with my son the whole time. Cause he could have took my son where and raped and killed him god forbid. But God was with my son the whole time. God bless that white man who help my son. After the Brooklyn Police Department contact my mother who live in 2162 Valentine Ave. Apt 7-C in the Bronx at the time of the incident. I'm glad my 7 yr. old son who is now 30 yrs. Old now. And have beautiful girls 2 yrs. 4 yrs. 7 yrs. And my 26 yr.old have a 7 yr. old also. I have 4 beautiful daughters. I always thank God for waking me up every morning when Raihem would read his bible sometime. He would never let me see which part of the bible he was reading you know why cause he was using the bible to hurt me. I didn't know that my 26 yr. old son father was reading this book in jail called art of seduction. A lot of men in jail reads that book. It tells men in jail how to tame and control their women. Raihem likes going to jail cause his boyfriend is there. I believe Raihem likes dick better than pussy cause Raihem got a lot of gay friends he hangs out with in midtown some of them were pick pockets are boosters. Why in the hell would he tell me that kind of shit. Unless you were sucking one of them. I got 12 yrs clean from smoking crack cocaine. I used to go to NA. I got keychains I been in 5 residential programs J. Cap, Phonix House, Project Return, 12 Detoxes people place and things will get you in trouble. If you forget where you came from my mother used to buy me crack cocaine in the early 90's. She said she rather buy it for me instead of me going on a rooftop somewhere and find my body the next day she use to let me smoke in the house. But never around my sons never. But my boys wasn't stupid either. I had took things from my sons when I was using but I'm glad my son forgave me. But they will never forget it. And neither will I. I wasn't proud of myself when I was using. I did not like myself. Raihem introduce me to crack cocaine when I was 24 yrs. Old. I never smoked newports cigarettes until the age 24. He used to take me to other women's house in Harlem and tell me that they were just his get high bubbies yeah right. I would remember a couple of times he would leave me in one crack house and be in another. I guess he was getting his dick sucked are he was sucking dick licking ass who knows. I remember he beat me in my head with one of my blk patent leather shoe all in my head. Cause he lie another time. Suppose to been going to get something to eat. He never came back to enter on that night. Guess what he had a bag of dope 2 bags crack and give dollars. Talking about get them some Chinese food to eat. I said I don't need your 5.00. I said the super gave me money to feed my son the super help me after Raihem got busted a week later. Good for his ass. I started fucking the Super to my building. I stop smoking crack. Went to my first detox, went to J.Cap as my first drug program. Cause I thought he believe in me he was full of shit too. After I left the program when the Super found out he beat me with a washing machine hose I was in pain for a week in a half. I had bruises all over my body that bastard knew I was smoking before he met me. He call his self beating me with washing machine hose would make me stop smoking.

A real muslim ain't dealing with no woman smoking crack to me he was a fake muslim. I been abused my creep as men all my life. I got molested at 5 yrs old right in my mother building by a family member and also at 5 yrs from the super who ran the building. Around 2008 Raihem and me would be out trying to get money. And he would bump into some his henchman this mother fucker would an coune me as his girlfriend or his friend. I could not believe he was telling them that shit. After carrying your son for 9 months and put up with his lying and cheating I should have earned the title this is my son's mother. I never heard that come out his mouth in the whole 26 yrs I've been with this creep. In 2004 I applied for SSI they denied me so I went for appeal they awarded me 18,000 welfare took the 5,000 and change that left me with 14,000 something. Raihem was locked up as usually on his sme Bib from 2002, when he came from up state from doing 6 yrs. I sent him 300.00 money order sent him some blk leather low cut tims. He did not appreciate it cause when got released 60 days later from doing 90 days. Bid he left the Tims with another inmates when he came out he had a pair of upstate converse's on. He gave them to one of his boyfriends ungrateful bastard. So when he seen my apartment he was hating. I bought me a bedroom set queen's size I paid 2,800, my living room set 1,195.00 dollars. Bought me two flat screens TV. A washing machine, air conditioner. Bought me 3 pairs of mauri shoes. He was hating as usual. He didn't compliment nothing I bought. I'm glad he was in jail when I got my money. Cause if he was out. He would have tried to rob me and go spend my money on another bitch. I don't think so, so one night I was sleeping. When I woke up he was knocking at the door so when I let him in I went back to my room and turned on my flat screen. It starting running. Now normally when I turn my TV there nothing wrong. So god told me to get up and look behind my TV the cable cord was hanging out. So I turned and looked at him I said why where you trying to steal my TV. He said I didn't touch your TV. Yeah right mother fucker. Cause when cable put the card in the back of your TV's they put them cords on tight. He's full of shit. He was planning on catching me sleep and he was going to dip with my flat screen in the middle of night. Now mind you my son was in my living room watching the other flat screen. So he could not go pass my son cause he was on his laptop. But check this the line I live on in 1898 Harrison Ave. Didn't have a fire escape. I had a backdoor so I would leave that as my storage closet so if he would have tried to take it out the back door. I would have woke-up cause he had to move them boxes I had there and I had 2 shopping carts there. So his Ass would have got caught. My mother used to call him a tall glass of water back in the late 80's and 90's I did not understand what she meant now I see then she would tell me I couldn't see the forest from the trees. Now I really see what she was talking about. Believe me if this book sells I coming out with another it wil be base on why young women in their late 20's call themselves mother. Anybody can lay down and have a baby that does not mean you are a mother. Real talk when that books come out maybe it will wake a lot of these young dumb mother up getting back to Raihem. One day back in the late 80's early 90's me and Raihem was getting high. My choice of drugs was always woolies. Never smoked the stem only woolies weed crack cocaine. I would smoke it in bamboo paper. Anyway my thing was while I was enjoying my woolie I liked to watch superfly. Now mind you Raihem is on his side of bed with his ash pipe his 2 bgs dope his new ports cigarettes. He would go in his pocket and pay me ten dollars. So he can order a x-rated movie. It got tiring while I smoking why do I have to look at stink funky cumming pussy or big blk penis in my face and he would keep rewinding to certain parts. I would ask him at times to fuck with his high. What are you really looking at the dicks or the pussy. I really believe it be the dicks. I thought he like the front but he like going through the back door. Around the time I met Raihem after he got raped in jail. One day Raihem house caught of fire the rumor was he set the fire. Cause he wanted his mother to move off of 184 street grand ave. Cause news spread fast while you in jail. While he was still locked up before the fire nigers already on the street heard about his rape before he got out. What a fag. He can beat on one call me all kinds of name. But he can't fight his way out of wet paper bag. I had a friend atleast I thought she was my friend. One night I came home from a comedy show at BB Q's n ford hammer. When I got to my building I look up cause lived on the 5th floor in the front of the building.

So I look up all my lights were out except for my bedroom. He had the music blasting real hard in the living room so he did not hear me come in. I crept in my bedroom I pushed the door open there he is on his fucking knees, eating out this crack head baron. I could not believe my eyes he had that raggedy snag toothball head snunk on my 2,800 bedroom set. The bedroom smell like ass. I don't know whether it was his ass or hers. He jumped up started punching me all in my face and pull some from letting my African sister put box braids in my hair. I thought me and him was going to chill when I came back from getting my hair doe. But It did not work out that way. While I trying to stop him from hitting me the bitch got her funky tong on and these dirty funky cut-off shorts back on. That bitch ran and then he let me go. And got dress and left. I did not see him for 3 days. Word he was at the dirty crack apartment. I would go knocked on the door. She would sneak to her peep hole then creep back to the creep. She had in their was Raihem. God don't like ugly what goes around come around. Believe that shit. As I said again and again I been writing jokes for a couple of years. I started writing jokes in 97 up until 2012. And I know I'm a funny character I make people laugh everywhere I go. I remember I had the D Train and the 4 Train laughing when I got off the train they were clapping for me. This was on different occasions. I'm not scared of no audience, scare money don't get no money I wanna take my negative attitude and turn it into a positive. I'll be a bad mother fucker I tired of men abusing women treating them like a piece of dirt. I got a serious issue with men beating and raping women. Violating our bodies what give them the right who died and left them boss.

I liked old school music from the 70's I grew up on that music. So sometimes I would turn the oldies channel 857. He would say why you are listening to that sorry ass music. I said you and me were raised on this music so what bitch I don't wanna hear that shit. So he said if I don't turn he will throw something at my flat screen. So I would turn to the rap channel just to keep the peace. When he went out I hope he would never come back in 2010 I got my wrist broken on Fordham Road. I enter a beauty supply store to buy me a perm. The floor was wet, so I fell hard. Whereas I had to get metal in my right wrist for the rest of my life. When I fell my wrist bend backward. I had to go to surgery the next morning. Raihem said he will call me in the morning. Cause he had to go t meet his man to see about a job, yeah right. Come to find out my neighbor told me she spotted Raihem entering some white men car. And they drove off. He didn't see Raihem until 4:00 am that morning. When this white man drop him in front of the building. I still to this day wonder what that was about. I know what it was Raihem was selling his ass for crack or heroin. I hope and pray Raihem don't come a victim of HIV cause he fucks anybody if the bitch can't walk he will drag her but when I caught him eating baron's cunt on my bed adter I tell y'all a little more about

WANDA REYNOLDS

Raihem, I closing on his ass. I remember back when I lost my apartment me and sons had to leave the building cause my sister rest her soul. Her and her man would fight over men in the building over my sister was tall black stallion like her big sis anyway me and my two handsome sons who stand 6 and a half, 6 tall.

We move to a hotel on 144 street a Lenox Ave. I didn't want Raihem with us. So when we got off the train at his edge comb. I told my boys to start running down the hill. So I'm jogging behind them Raihem had bad feet and I have bad feet. So he said wanda wait for me I said fuck you niger. So I kept on jogging my sons was all ready at the bottom of the hill. So now they are waiting for me to cross them across the street this fool started throwing bottles at me while I'm jogging down the hill. I kept going got my sons on the other side of the street. I pick up my 4 yr old and 8 yr old was right with me. So when I got to security I told them not to let Raihem in the building cause he's not on my lease. So they did exactly that fuck Raihem. Raihem can beat ass for all I care one day I went to see Raihem in 2005 up state Marcy Correctional facility. So I thought I was going with the other women in the visiting room. No one of the C/o's said Ms. Reynolds you have come to the pyschrtri part of the jail. When I go to see Raihem he was sitting in a chair all spaced out guess what Raihem got for the rest of his life. O well you have to find out in my next book. Aries vs. Aries.

I have been around women all my life that were getting abuse by their husbands or boyfriend. And I really sick and tired of that bullshit. Now I'm telling you about some abusive relationships about women I met over the years I heard their stories. Some of the things I heard brought water to my eyes. I'm tell you 5 stories, I'm not using these women real names in the book.

I lost my section 8, in Dec.2011. So I had to put my furniture in storage. And that where it still is. I'm not losing my storage wars on cable how they pop your storage unit. If you do not pay well they won't break mines. Anyway after 12 yrs. On section 8. I went to this women shelter right around the corner from where I live for 12 yrs. Anyway I stayed there for 3 months they found one housing within that 3 months to a brand new building in the Fordham Road section. I refused it the building had too many rules on the building. My son will be coming home soon. And I'm not leaving my 26 yr old in the street when he comes home. I love my two handsome and I got 4 beautiful granddaughter one in Brooklyn Tyliyah Reynolds 7 yrs old. She is my first granddaughter. The last time I see Tyliyah she was 2 yrs old now she is 7 yrs old the mother took her from me and my son when she was 2. But that's okay cause I really believe God is going to bring Tyliyah back to me and my son.

Now I got 3 grand girls down in Fayetteville, North Carolina. Another 7 yr old her name is Heavenly then a

4 yr old named Honesty then my 2 yr old Harmony. I love all 4 of my girls and I be glad when Tyliyah see her 3 cousins Down South. Okay enough of that.

After I did not take the apartment in the Fordham Area DHS send me downsouth. To stay with my older son who is 30 yrs old and my daughter in law now mind you I never been to the south. When I got off that bus at Fayetteville my son was there to pick me up. Him and his girls I love it down south. I did not want to come back to NYC for what anyway I met 5 abused women down there. I was hanging out with every day. I stayed a month. I witness 3 of the abuse relationship. All of them want me to let the world know what it is to be abused. Remember I'm not using their real names. Here we go pay close attention.

1. The first sister is 52 yrs old. Her name is Lacey. When I met my friend Lacey. I calling her my friend cause I can I'd with some of the things I seen her husband do to her in front of my face. Her husband is a fucking drunk all he did while I was down there the eight 8 months was beat on Lacey. Morning, noon and night. Lacey went to the hospital 3 times cause of this bastard. Lacey do not drink all she did was smoke a bunt with me every now and then. Then her 2 grand daughter's would play with my 3 girls. Now he's one of them working alcoholic everytime he comes home. She got his dinner ready. His bath water ready.

What more you want motherfucker. He would always come from work talking shit all in front of my grandkids and their 2 grandkids bitch get your fucking pot head ass in the trailer bitch and get my food and my bathwater ready. Atleast the mother fucker washed his ass on a regular anyway she got up and went in there and did exactly what she was told until one day Lacey snapped on that day. She left the girls playing with my girls so I remember Lacey would always knock on my son's trailer looking for me. But my son would tell me mom please do not get in that shit. Cause Mrs. Lacey and him always go through that mom. I said I'm getting in that from the oldest of my youngest Terrell. Anyway Lacey go inside. I hear them pulling on her hair she telling that drunken bastard to get off her hair. He let her hair go, now's he's calling her all out her name. Mind you while she heating up his food. She is boiling water now he is steady talking shit at the table. Still drinking a beer. He had cases of them 211 beer in her fridge. She calls me in her trailer one morning after he went to work. I couldn't believe all them un opened cans of 211 beers. That why this drunk got what he got that evening. You would think Lacey would let me know what she was going to do this man. She told me one afternoon we sitting there laughing and joking she came out the clear blue. One day and said I might go to jail one day for really hurting this man. I said it ain't worth it just call the police. She said wanda you know how many times I called the sheriff on this bastard. Round 12 times she said every complaint is on record. So shit I said well do what you have to do. Now getting back to her heating up his dinner now the water is boiling hot. While she is fixing his food. She sits at the table with him, so she told him she is leaving and taking their grandkids. He said bitch where will you go nobody wants you. You will never be shit look at you you are has been. So now she is laughing in his face while he is eating. Next thing yo know he got up and came around the table and he grab herby her neck. And said what so funny mother fucker. She said you bitch he let her neck go. Which he should not have did. He threw her against the kitchen floor with all his might. So my son called me I think Lacey and will is going at it again. All I heard from her trailer door was you fuckin bitch I'm gonna kill you bitch. Lacey got up ran to the stove threw the hot water straight in that bastard face then she had a cup of bleach and threw that after he was rubbing his face. So his skin was peeling. When the sheriff came to Lacey trailer you know what the Sheriff said to Lacey when they pulled up on her lawn. Don't Lacey we got if from here. My girl did ot spend one day in jail cause she had over a dozen reports on him at the pricent see men like to beat on us make us feel like it our faults when they fuck up they try to make us have a low self esteem about our self not me I know I'm tall black stallion. When I get dress I'm not letting no more abusive men in my world no more. I can do badly myself Lacey if you buy this book. I see you when I come back to Fayetteville North Carolina, cause I wanna get me a house with a big backyard. So my 4 beautiful girls can spend time with their grandmother. I could have been a woman to help abusive women get through their abuse with these creepy ass relationshit.

2. The second sister I'm getting ready to tell you about it had me in tears cause while I was in Fayetteville for them 8 months I heard and seen how men treat the women like dogs. Well her namee is Destiny. Destiny is 32 years old. She had one daughter. But she lost her daughter to the foster agency because she wasn't talking care of her business. When it came to her 6 months old daughter Destiny and her baby's father was selling heroin and using it. Leaving the baby in the trailer all by herself. So me and my nosey self heard the baby crying one morning. I told my son Tromell you don't hear that baby crying. He said mom stay out of it. It's none of your business. I go and knock on the door. I get no answer the trailer door was a jar the door half crack where you can see inside.

So the baby was still crying I go inside. Now my son is watching as I go in. I go get the baby out of this dresser drawer. The baby is hollering, soaking wet there was no pampers left for the baby there was no milk so my two year old wore pampers at aht time. She better not be wearing pampers now cause I trained her ass before I left fayetteville NC. Anyway getting back to the baby. So I bought the baby out that dirty ass trailer. Shit I thought my daughter in law trailer. Shit hers was paradise compared to Destiny trailer. Anyway I got some of my 2 yr old baby wipe put a pamper on the little boom boom. Here goes my son now being that you went in that trailer without permission mom what do you plan on doing with that baby. I'm going to sit here and give this baby some milk. The baby was 6 month old my son said mom you can't give that baby regular milk. I said watch me. What else was I going to give her that baby was glad to get that warm bottle of milk. I lotion down the baby my 7 yr old heavenly went in her little drawer and there was clothes to small. She got one of her sister undershirts with the snap. Between the legs to hold the pampers in place. So now I sitting in the yard asking myself what should I do. Call the sheriff or wait on Destiny and her man. Here they come driving up the road in this raggedey hoopdy. High as a kite. Destiny ran right pass me. Hello Ms. Wanda talking about she has to use the bathroom. Mind you I still got the baby in my arms the baby is fast asleep. Sucking her thumb now her man is getting out the car. Atleast he notice the baby I said I heard the baby crying. If you don't mind I went in the trailer to check on the baby cause she was crying he said thanks Ms. Wanda so now Destiny comes out the trailer sreaming where is my daughter he got her man you stupid bitch. Can you see Miss Wanda is holding her she said O shit. I didn't even see you holding my daughter. So he explaining what happened so now my son's goes back in his trailer that left me and Destiny on the lawn cause her trailer was right next to my son's trailer was right noext to my son's trailer. Now my friend Lacey was 2 trailers a away. Anyway here goes Destiny I know Ms. Wanda please do not start preaching to me. About my screwed up life. I said Destiny. It's not about you light now it's about your 6 month old daughter what are you going to do about her. I'm going to get some help and go in a program. She said she is trying to kick my drug habit. I said herion is not good for you to be using that poison you just killing you self slowly. She said yeah Ms. Wanda you are right. So I asked her while we were talking on the law. He's calling her tellin when you finish talking to Ms. Wanda look in the car I left the bag in the glove compartment. She said okay daddy she stops talking to me. Runs to the car get the bag out the glove compartment. So I asked her what's in the bag she said me and his works. So she asked me to watch the baby for a little while so I told her I'll keep the baby in my son's trailer for a couple of days. I'm sure my daughter in law wouldn't mind. Destiny and the creep of a father was happy to hear that mind you my son is asking me mom I know you love kids and everything. But you cant not get involve with that mom. I said Tromell I'm already involved I got involved when I heard that baby crying in that trailer that's when I got involved son that was that. So Destiny said Ms. Wanda later me and my man is going to make some money to buy the baby some milk and pampers I said Destiny if I wait on you to get some milk and pampers list. So I took her baby my son took me to the supermarket in Fayetteville and I got her baby two cans of similac with iron. And a pack of pampers newborns to be 6 months old her baby could have been a little heavier. All she was feeding the baby was milk, milk, milk. When she had in the fridge the baby need water also. So I got a bottle put a little sugar and water warm it up that baby torn that water up. The baby was dehydrated. Some young women should not have kids just because you have a baby that does not mean you are a women. You have to earn that title after Destiny got through getting high she comes out the trailer nogging and slobbing out the side of her mouth here he come out the trailer. Talking about they will be back in an hour. They going to get money to feed their baby. Yeah right. Y'all going to set the next fix. They never came baby that night, Destiny came back two days later talking about her baby father Roger, got busted selling oxycotton. O well I said god did that for a reason. God knows he was bringing you down. Anyway me and Destiny was talking. I told her I use to use drugs in the early 80's Raihem introduce me to crack cocaine. I got 10 yrs clean all I do now is smoke a blunt every once in a while. Shit what wrong with a blunt. O well anyway I asked her straight talk now that he in jail where god put him what are you going to do with your life before it to late. She said Ms. Wanda to tell you the truth. I glad you kept my baby for me and I'm glad you did not call the authority. I callingmy oldest sister in Charleston South Carolina. And she coming to get into somebody's detox and then I'm going to rehab. I said good for you Destiny. So I let her use my cellphone she called her big sister. Her sister had to drive a few hours before hse got to Fayetteville NC. When she did arrive. I had the baby Destiny was nice fresh and got clean got in her sister red Hummer and went and got her life together. God willing destiny I'm coming back to the south to become a stand up comedian all my jokes are on men how they treat the women, they supposedly are in love with you yeah right niger and I hope to see you at one of mine shows. God Bless you baby and take of your baby get into Destiny what wants out of life.

3. Now this young woman my son introduce me to while I was visiting in Fayetteville for 8 month. Her name is Latoya. The reason he said that he liked Latoya cause she reminded her of his cousin moaster. Cause my son would hang out with mooster brother sometimes. Now one day Latoya came knocking on my daughter in law trailer. Cause she needed a pamper for her 2 yr old daughter. So I said my son and his wife aint have at the moment. She said my daughter needs a pamper. I said well I'm not giving you my granddaughter last pampers. So she said what I'm going to do. So I asked her do you have any old clean rags in you trailer that way you can make her a pamper out of the rags. So she did just that. She didn't have no safety pins. So I gave her two she said thank you. So now I closing the trailer door. Cause now I have to attend to my 3 granddaughter fix their bathwater. Get out the summer clothes underwear. What were they going to put on after their bath. So she said I be back over later. So I closed the door around two hours later. I get a hard knock on my sons trailer door. I do not see no one so I look down and there was

ere 2 yr old on the bottom step just standing there
I said what happen where is mommie she said she
got in a car said she was going to the store. So I
took the 2 yr old inside now my grandkids asking
me questions. So we all came outside on the grass
they running up and down the yard. So I calls my
son's job. Cause he works at the army base. He
answers his phone at the third ring. I told him
about his friend and her 2 yr old daughter. He
said he just stay and help them out I said Tromell
what I suppose to do for this girl and her child. I
not no guidance counslor. So he said mom act like
one. I have to go back to work. So I asked her who
lives with you she said just me and daughter. So I
said wher is the father at. She said he back in jail
again. I said what did he do to get in jail again.
They caught him stealing someone's purse at the
bus stop with him. But it was an off duty sheriff
helping some old Lady aboard the bus. That when
she seen him reaching for someone's pocket book.
And she said he is gonna be there for a couple of
years so I said what your gonna do now she said
Ms. Wanda I'm going back to New York and ask
my family up in New york to help raise my two
year old daughter. So I can go get my life together.
I do not want no jail bird pick pocket around me
and my daughter. So before I left to come back to
New York Latoya family came from New york to
get her and her daughter and Latoya if you buy

this book remember Ms. Wanda from Fayeteville NC God Bless you and yours Latoya all the time. I was listening to your story about your baby father life. I wanna tell you I was in love with a pick pocket for 26 yrs. Raihem did not love me out them whole 26 yrs. But them days is over. I have to keep on keeping on. I'm not letting no more miserable phoney ass peope join my circle. Only way you could be in my circle is you had to go through the cause I went through for the 26 yrs. That probably why my son told me about Latoya. Cause her man was a pickpocket also. But it's all good son love you thanks for the heads up. I will never mess with another pick pocket again. If you love something set it free. If it was meant it will come back. If not fuck you move with your life. Life goes on all abusive men to stay locked up in jail. Now the reason I said all abusive men should stay lock up is because this is next story I witnessed with my own eyes. I knew this Libra age 46 yrs old. Now she said I can talk about her on stage. When I go tell my jokes anyway I'm talking about her in this book. Now I met her like the 5th month down there. Like I'm gonna call her Libra. Now Libra got thirteen boyfriends. Yes 13 boyfriends at least that what she said. I believe her cause I got to meet around 6 of these sorry ass mother fuckers and I mean sorry first of all that is embarrasing to even tell someone you got 13 boyfriends. I told her you is a fucking hog. That why men aint got respect for women cause of your stink funky ass. Let me tell you about this hoe and I mean hoe. Now like I said I met all of her six boyfriends never met the other seven and I really don't wanna meet them. Now she do not call them by there names. She calls them by numbers.

Now let me tell you about the No.6 he is paranoid schizophrenic lives in Fayetteville NC in this own house but this skank stay in a trailer with Dino. Dino, he's a very nice person. He met this skank at a motel. When one of daughter like 3 yrs old. Now when daughter is like 19 yrs old. Now her and her daughter stay with this man name Dino. Now he got an honorable discharge from the army. This man was a descent person. Before her stink ass came alone. This pill head dope head crack head bitch don't have no type of income coming in. all she get is food stamps. No cash. When you are a single person down south all you will get is food stamps. But mind you her daughter get a job. She be begging her own daughter for money. Her daughter don't like giving her money cause her daughter knows she is fucking crack head. So she claim she do not smoke crack yeah right. I know a crack head when I see one. Cause I use to smoke crack 10 yrs ago. I went to NA been in detoxes, drug programs but by the grace of God I take it one day at a time. And don't forget where I come from now getting back to Dino, like I said he a good guy. But with the wrong woman. She smokes cause Dino smokes crack. He's 53 yrs old weight about 110 pounds 54 inches tall. She always calling this man out his name. Now that is trailer she and her daughter are free loading her daughter do not pay rent nor do her funky ass. She a straight alcoholic and crack head. Every time he gets his 3 checks from the army every month his rent is always paid on time. He pays his cable bills every month. His land lady get her rent every month directly to her bank account. So he's good. His sister is her payee. I don't blame her for protecting her brother money from that bitch. Let me tell you what she will do. He does not give her none of his money. Cause he said she does not satisfy his sexual needs. After he get high off his drugs. He wants a little sexual healing she do not have time for him. So when he get on his cellphone and call up one of his lady friends she gets mad telling him she ain't leaving. He would tell her being that you ain't giving me no pussy you might as well it the bricks. Cause I need my privacy. All they drink all day is coors beer and them cheap ass 211 beer plus she told me she takes pertset pills and crush them up and sniff the pill. Now this jealous cock blocking bitch is all charge up and ready to go. So she was telling when Dino lady friend arrives. So when the girl came in the trailer. This bitch told his girlfriend to leave talking about ain't going be no crack smoking in here so him and that skank started fighting. She pull a knife out her pocket book. The lady friend got her pocket book and left. Next thing I know that skank ran towards Dino with her knife stab that man right in his neck. Blood was shooting everywhere so the lady friend heard glass breaking this bitch was busting out all the man windows in his trailer, all because he wanted to be with someone. Who was willing to do whatever he wanted. When she pushed the trailer door open Dino was lying on the floor in his own blood. The skank was still in the trailer when to sheriff's car arrive they threw that skank to the ground. And hand cuffed her ass. She was trying to fight the police back. They sprayed her like 3 times that crack head bitch was still coming at them until one police officer hit that bitch real hard in her head. They got Dino to the hospital, if they would have not got him to the hospital when they did he would have died. They locked her up and from I hear she still is in jail. See where drugs can lead you jails, institute, death drugs kill. Now see if any of your 13 boyfriends come visit you bitch they probably got that chick in a padded cell with a straight jacket that bitch I crazy. Dino don't worry you find you a good woman one day just leave the drugs alone. I said I wasn't talking my son father no more. I was going to save it for my 3rd book, cause my second book will be called Young mothers in their late 20's should not have kids. If they can't take care of them. I'm tell you a little bit about someone real close to me I aint using her name. But you know like I said some young girls in there twenty's should not have kids now this person is 24 years old and have a badass 3 year old girl. And I mean this 3 year old girl is a badass no manners whatsoever. She spits she curses and she will pull her butt cheeks and she will pull her vagina apart and tell you to suck her pussy. She will pick up heavy objects and try and throw it at you. And my 24 niece I'm talking that her 3 year old daughter and all she do is drink her Henessy smokes her weed, smokes her newports and let her daughter just tear the house apart all the mother do is fuck all kind of Jamaicans. That skank dank got a highschool diploma, ain't trying to use it I remember one night this bitch call me 3 am in the morning talking about her daughter was sick and need to go to the hospital. Her temperature was 101. So she call the cab to come get her and daughter. Now she got to Jacobi Hospital around 3:30 am. So I told the dummy to call me every now and then so I know what is going on. She was saying if they do not cal her soon I'm leaving the hospital. I said you can not leave until that daughter of yours see a doctor, well if they don't call her soon I'm leaving. I said girl it is a waiting process. She leaves out the hospital 30 minutes later here comes the police at her door they were going to lock her ass up for leaving the hospital see why I said young mother should not have kids that what is gonna be in my second book. Young mother's in there 20's should not have kids. I wrote a little about the second book. I repeat the next book will be about young mothers in their 20's should not have kids.

I wanna talk about how ACS takes people's kids from their real parents and turn them over to crack heads parents. Mean why your child is getting sexually abused by his or her foster parents. The reason I'm speaking about ACS is because they took my kids from me at the ages of 3 years old and 7 yrs old cause of that bastard Raihem. He took my seven year old with him to Manhattan to pick pockets. After he got the money he is taking my 7 year old in all kinds of houses on 119 street. You had to pay two dollars to get in the matter he got tired of my son he put my son on the D. Train I used to tell my son when we would ride the train to my mother's house we would always get off at 183rd street. But he was on the D.Train going downtown. My son was sleeping on the train and this whiteman woke my son up and ask him was lost. He said yes sir he took my son to the coney island police station. He could have took my son somewhere and Raihem. But God was with my son. Thanks to the white man.

I had a girlfriend. She used to smoke crack. She had 3 girls ages 8,10,12 and she had 2 boys 6,7 and she had 3 different baby's daddy, 2 was on crack. 1 had a descent job. He worked for the sanitation department. He been working there like 8 yrs. He was good to his 2 sons. His son loved their father thanks to his sons they were very special to him. But he do not live with the boys because mother is still using and he's in court right now fighting to get his sons away from their crack addicted mother everytime he would come pick his kids for the weekend he notice his sons clothes were disappearing. So she said he didn't mention to the boys mother yet. He said he would give her the benefit of the doubt until lone day. He said he had just drove up on her. And she was selling his clothes to the next door neighbor. He was telling me Wanda I can't believe what he was seeing. So he said he jump out the car. Ran up on her so he asked her why is you out here selling our kids clothes to your neighbors. He said when he walk up to her she was twinking and her eyes was big as two marble. He had called the police then ACS came. He wanted him ass arrested but his two sons were begging him not to lock mommy up the 7 yr old month. These kids are very smart and sharp these days. He went to court and granted his custody of his two sons. Now her second baby daddy had the 8 yr old girl now her father and mother. Be making there 8 yr old daughter sell candy to door everyday just together ma and pa crack. Then she packs bags in the supermarket on the weekend until one day her teacher had came to the supermarket over the weekend. Up in sound view projects and asked her why haven't she been coming to school cause she has to work for her mother, the teacher asked what kind of work she said selling candy door to door on the weekend and working in the supermarket packing bag. The father that his sons taking out the house called ACS find the other 3 girls in the house. There was no food no milk juice nothing. All you see all around her house garbage, roaches it was a mess ACS got all kids out safe and sound.

Now AC wanted to put him in a program. So where are you going back ACS will have somewhere to help you.

Now mind you my friend I know she has a 3 yr old daughter 3 years old mind you. She spits she curses she will spread her little ass cheeks and tell you to kiss her ass the will open her clit and tell you to suck her pussy. She spits she curses like a sailor, my niece acts like she scare of her own daughter Angela do anything she want. She stick both her middle finger at you. She know how to put curse words to good here are some of the words she might said when you get her real she will go find the heavy things to throw at you. She pisses ass through my mother house, my niece one day right after I came back from Fayetteville NC I was sitting in my mother living room my niece moved her barnall lick up her hard doo-doo and then it missed it was one of them hard doo-doo like a snow ball. Don't you know that little mother through it at me. I called my niece in the living. I said look what your fucking daughter did asking me to clean it up I said you crazy bitch. My mother fucking daughter chews on toilet paper they both should go see about some SSI. Then I know my friend she get her period she leaves her nasty bloody pads behind radiator. Why would you leave your bloody under wear behind the steam pipe that is nasty then me and my friend got into a fight at my other friend house. She was trying to show off in front of her man. Was playing around with her daughter she don't listen to mother. Now she know that girl ain't got no respect they need to come and take a look at the dirty apartment. My friend leave her grandmother house dirty she does not care all I see that bitch is let your daughter be disrespectful to people who only that girl or something else time. Want she let her daughter 3 years old run around all days with no manner. I said put a pamper she don't like pamper. I do not care what she said. I do not look right for 2 men watching a 3 yr old running around she keep the house real dirty roaches everywhere I know the lady how she stays with got high blood pressure. Grunt my mother ain't going to be forever some young women this hoe already got a case with ACS. She keep playing and acting like she don't know her ears from her elbow I told my friend you already got ACS now mind you a little girl of mine is missing her name is Tyliyah Desiree Reynold. She lives in Williamsburg houses in Buswick. Now mind you me and my son's did not see my granddaughter and his son. The last time me and my granddaughter see Tyliyah Reynolds she was only 2 years old. Now Tyliyah is 7 yrs old. Tyliyah got 3 girl cousins down in Fayetteville NC and Tyliyah never, ever seen her cousin. Last time I seen my granddaughter it was on her birthday I bought her a God change and ring they were bet you she do not have them gold cross now nor the ring. I hope and pray bring my granddaughter to me and my son one day I heard she has another baby girl good for God bless you. But I to see my granddaughter she already go ABC with her son. In the foster system. Her grandmother got custody cause she could handle her son. She would leave him in the house and go hang out and her grandmother got custody. Why me and my son Terrell can't get to see Tyliyah when we want I went out to Williams Burghouse. Went to the housing office. They would not give me no information for my granddaughter me and son missed 5 yrs of her life. Well I plan on doing stand up mic around 2013 on me 50th birthday God spare

my life some people should not have kids. Then one day I
see this lady whipping a 20 month of baby n her carriage,
cause she want a juice box her mother slapped that baby.
Her print was on the baby face some people not have kids.
Tyliyah grand needs to see you. Remember I used to call
you coo gee moo gee that was grandma use to call you
Tyliyah Desiree Reynolds what an ugly name Desiree and
it was her fault her and my son broke-up first fo she was
using my son the hold time. She had a man in jail and a
son from this man. She would always tell my son. That
her baby father was coming out of jail so what about my
son. She put him out so my son came to stay with me.
And way she mad cause her friend had a crush on him he
had sex with both of them mind you they are cousins. She
got mad cause Terrell was getting his dick wet shit the one
that brought that swingging In the bedroom her moms
got custody of my granddaughter using her SSI money for
her whatever she uses it for Tyliyah grandma still searching
for your mother can keep on playing games cause Tayann
what goes around comes around.

ACS

I know you know that some mother should not have kids
cause I knew this puerto rican name Carmen. She have 3
boys, she was on herion. She would leave her kids with all
kinds of people in her building complex. She comes back
days at time mind you mother lived in the building
complex also she is a working church going women. She

would go check on her brand kids every now and then cause her and daughter did not get along. Cause her mother did like seeing her daughter killing her self. Carmen had a boyfriend name Jimmy Mac. Jimmy Mac was a pimp for 10 years but carmen mother did not know her son in law was a pimp until the oldest son was telling his grandmother don't want to live with his mother and father no more he does not feel safe around them so his grandmother took temporarily custody of her grandsons and her daughter hug her mother and told her she was going to detox and then rehab and her husband said he not ready to stop using drugs. I knew this guy Bobby he live in the bronx, NY and bobby kept on using drugs and until day they were tearing down a vacant two story building and find bobby cold and he was blue. To all my fans reading this book. I got high early 80's. my son father Raihem started me smoking crack at the age 24 yrs old. I stop using crack cocaine 12 years ago and I'm proud to say, I am living to tell the world that it feels good when you can wake up in the morning drug free what it was for me growing up watching my real father abuse drugs and then abuse my mother and her kids my mother hated my real father so much she made him sleep on a cox in the living room he was not a loud in her bedroom no more. And when he got hungry and my mother would charge him for something to eat. He did not trust my mother. He would ask her to taste the food first. I've met Raihem like I said in the early 80's cause I had our son in 1985. But the reason I speaking of this creep again in because our son is now 26 years old and he has a 7 year old daughter Tyliyah Desiree Reynolds she lives in Brooklyn NY with her mother I haven't seen Tyliyah Reynolds since she was 2 yrs old. I miss 5 yrs old my daughter life. I call her my daughter cause she's mine granddaughter. I love and miss her dearly all I know is she is in William Bridge Projects. Now Tyanna and my son had a relationship but when she bought her cousin in the bedroom to join in after that that's the last time I seen my granddaughter now mine you that is Raihem granddaughter also but he never acted like a grandfather to my grand daughter he never spend time with her like I did. When I did she her out of them 2 years cause he is always in jail. Now he suppose to get out of jail Sept. 25,2012. Wow he ain't never gonna change he is now 49 years old. Still thinking he is 19 years old. Hating on his own son. He is very jealous of hs son. But I know for a fact my son is not only Raihem child in reality truly believe he has more kids out there. I put 2,000 on that. Cause he is a real dog. He worst then spo dog. He will fuck anything moving. If the chick can't walk he will drag her to their fucking spot. Now when he got raped in jail at age 16 yrs old. He looked like a real bitch then shit he had dark curly hair I mean curly like female and at that time he was around 130 pounds stood 6 feet at that time now he's 6'3" inches tall. Missing teeth in front. He lost 2 set of teeth mine you. Eating some bitch some funky stink pussy. He got this big nasty bump on his penis. He claims he was born like that yeah right niger. And mind you I just notice that bump a couple of years ago. Cause me and Raihem had not had sex in 2 yrs. Now mind you maybe I could be 3 yrs. Cause since he came back into me and my son life in 2002. From doing 6 yrs on some robbery charge he was on parole for that case when he got out in 2002 and still on the same case. Mind you he caught another case. So now his dumb ass is still on parole. I don't think he will never get off parole. He is a sad case poor excuse for a man. Now Raihem been going to jail since he was 12 years old. But I did not meet him until 16 years old at 41 west 184 street. Bronx NY. Now one day I'm coming in the building Raihem lived on the 1st floor. Raihem was a dust head when I moved in 41 west 184 street. Plus he was sniffing dope and hanging out in disco fever. Fucking everything that was not nail down. Now all through Raihem jail years old did not find out Raihem was Schizophrenia until age 46 yrs old one day I went to see Raihem at Marcy Correctional Facility. But when I got to Marcy Correctional Facility. I did not go wth all the other wives and girlfriends I had to get on a black van, and I was drove to Marcy Psychiatry so I'm asking questions as the CO's are taking me to see this ass. Anyway when I get there they me sit in this little room for maybe 20 minutes then here come Raihem dumbass throw a door that was connected to the room I was in. He standing there all crazy all medicated up. He looked like he was from another. So finally he sat down. I'm asking him do he have a psychiatrist he said yeah. So I told him I need to speak to him. He said he don't need to speak to him. O yes I do. Anyways one of the doctor that was in the visiting room got is doctor for me. Cause they do not have CO's in the visiting room only doctors. I guess if you act crazy they will stick your ass. His psychiatrist came like half hour later. He pull me to the size and told me what was going on with me. He said he didn't tell you I said tell me what. That he is schizophenia no. I said how long he been schizophrenia for a couple of years Mrs. Reynolds. So he said before the visit is over. I'm giving you so pamlets on it. So I when home read the pamplets and If a schizophrenia person male or female. Will get horny and fuck the world and I hate to say it but all he is going to do when he get out is go get his bumpy nasty dick suck. Fuck bitch. Smoke crack and get a bag of dope. He thinks that cool, the shit he be doing after a man hit 40 yrs old that suppose to get a test in their ass to make suer he does not have cancer but knowing hm he ain't gonna get it done. He will said I don't want no doctor looking in my ass. Well shit you did not say that at sixteen and I remember he use to hang out sometime with gay boosters. Talking about he ain't on it like that. Yeah right Raihem. Tell that to someone who do not know your funky stink cheating ass. Remember you went out one day bitch with underwear bitch and come back you ain't had on no underwear. Remember that niger. You are a very pitiful person. You never loved me or my son nor your granddaughter. But we will be together again one day. Me Tyliyah and her father. I wanna know why you did not tell me you were schizophrenia. I still loved and cared about you even though you didn't care about me from day one. But that okay I'm good. I rather be by myself anyway. I don't want no none kevin's. let alone another Aries hell to the NO. at one time I really loved and cared about Raihem even with his mental illness. But if he don't stay on his medication Raihem will be a victim of HIV the reason I say that is Schizophrenia men will have sex with anyone who comes along. Now like I said and I will say it again. Raihem got fucked in his ass at age 16 on Riker's island and he was also washing out niger dirty draws and funky socks now that was when he was 16. Well to me Raihem came institutionalize cause this punk been going to jail from 16 yrs old. To the age he is now. It's a damn shame. Raihem went to Walton HS and it sad to say he never went. He was busy cutting classes and picking pockets smoking dust sniffing dope at a very early age 12 yrs old. He had a pr of shoes the bottoms were all gone so he had to wear carboard in his shoes. Poor Raihem, yeah right fuck Raihem. Thanks to him this happen in 2010 on Fordham RD. in the Bronx I got 10 yrs clean from smoking crack cocaine and he's the one who introduce me to crack cocaine age 24 yrs.old. never smoked cigarettes until 24 yrs. Old. Thank Raihem and one day I just got tired of shoplifting that how I was supporting my drug habit. Back in the early 80's my mother used to buy me crack and let me smoke n her apartment instead of me being on a rooftop with some strange niger. And cut my throat God for bid. So she would buy my crack sometimes. It's nothing to brag about. But it is what it is. Now getting back to me saying Raihem might be an HIV is he do not straighten up his life.

Without taking his meds. He will go smoke crack get a bag dope. Go fuck on of them stunk scaccy wags on 183rd st. lay up them hoes until he get tired of them. He will ride his funky ass down to 119 street. Lay up down there with them dumb broads, now when he get his SSI back them nasty bitches will be right there in his back pocket getting every penny. Cause that's the ass he like being and believe me when I tell you he will be a victim cause Raihem came back to me and my son in 2002. Me and Raihem stop having sex cause there was never no love making in my bedroom. Raihem stop fucking me in 2008 but I still let him stay cause he was getting his SSI and he was looking out every now and then are if he get lucky he might come up with a wallet. But I would take bubble baths with candles around the tub. When he was home sometime and if I was in the bath are shower he would come wash my back are something. Are if I'm taking a shower he would come in. But sometime I did not want him in the bathroom with me cause he was a fake phony mother fucker. When he did get in he is hogging up all the water trying to use my doves soap are sometime would use one of bodywashes. Cause I had every fragrance of my dresser. Remember I was a booster. I got all my toiletress for free. Must keep that ass clean inside out. At I know I do. Love soap and water all day long even a douche. Some women don't douche let alone brush there teeth. But Raihem don't care. One day he had the nerve to tell me he can't really get hard with my pussy. Cause it's so clean he says he like when it smells, cause the smell turns him on.

So I told him I'm not doing nothing with you anyway I already know how he felt about me a long long time agao. He rather be around funky pussy. Well he can stay will all them funky bitches and they know who they are and I went a took all kinds of STD test last year 2010 and 2011 at Bronx Lebnon Hosp. cause Raihem got this big nasty bump on his penis. Talking about he was born with that. I do not remember seeing that bump back in the days. You know how this bump looks. If you go to the medical doctor and when he or she calls you in their office. They might have post of the water. Telling you about all kinds of diseases. Well you know the syllis chart. Well he got something like that on penis. After all by him being rape he like getting fucked in the ass I been with Raihem. All the time he went to city jails. And upstate jails and a lot of men up in them jails be fucking other men in jail. Then got a woman coming to see them and as soon as the fucking visit is over. He go Raihem and his crew he run with eating each other penis and fucking in the ass. I was messing with this other tall glass water, I ain't gonna mention his name he be in another one of my books. But let me tell what he did one day he went to jail and came hime with braids in his hair I asked him who did his hair he said one of his mans. I said oh he said why you said it like that. I just said oh. I would always do what Raihem wanted cause he would always promise me that he would do all kinds of things to me in the bedroom. But it never came one day he said he would eat my pussy but he said he never said it he is a liar. Cause I had letter from jail with him saying that. But its okay. I got it don't anyway niger. You probably can't eat pussy anyway. Raihem jealous cause I got 10 yrs clean and everytime he get busted and go to jail. He want me to stop doing what I doing to run see his funky ass talking about he wanna shine in jail. Go in the yard niger the sun will shine on that bald head of your. Now he is 49 yrs old still thinking he is his 20's hating on his son. I really Raihem got kids all over. Cause schizophrenia males will have sex with all kinds of women. I really believe sold his ass to other men. I really believe that I'm explain why I think so. One day raihem parole officer mandated him to an upstate rehab in Albany NY for 30 days. Raihem only stayed 12 days talking about he miss me and he wanna come home. Well I told Raihem if you get up and leave out that rehab your dumbass is on your own so he said he was leaving right after he get his last meal, dinner.

While he was eating dinner his counselor called me and told me Raihem was talking about leaving and the counselor said if he leaves he has to find his own means of transportation and he has to let his parole offices know that he left. Raihem lucky cause it was after 6:00 pm. When he left and it was the weekend, so he couldn't get in touch with Raihem parole officer,a nd he calls me back. I asked him how are you going to get pass the bus driver talking about he going to ask someone to pay his fare. Well had quarters cause he kept calling me every 10 minutes talking about he cant get on the bus. So I said how are you going to get back talking about he is going to hitch hike. So you gonna hitchike all the wayy from Albany NY to the Bronx. Now mind you when he did reach 1898 harrison Ave. Bronx NY it was exactly 1:00am. He come with his friend radio. So here I am thanking radio for going to get him all the way from Albany. So I said damn radio is a good friend to come pick his ass up. Radio said I didn't pick him up. I had know gas so I'm asking Raihem how he got back to NY he said well talk about it later. I said know who brought you back to NY he claims he called on of his home boys. So I'm asking his name. Talking about you don't know the person. I said try me. What is his name he never told me. Cause he sold his ass to another man that like men that who drove him home. Another person that like what they do to each other. His boyfriend came to picking up. And he came with money now when he left for the program he had no money. Sold his ass.

Now I was married to another man in 1999 until 2002, I divorce him cause Raihem came home talking about who gave you permission to get married. Anyway he was a creep like Raihem. I met him in 99. Cause I was homeless and he was homeless. Me and him would sleep in parks. Hospitals trains. The reason I'm telling y'all about this one I married. Cause he is a creep like Raihem. He's a momma's boy. Everytime we got into an argument he would call his momma. He spit food in my face. He beat me in my head one day. Cause he was a booster like me so me and him would go boosting everyday. So one day we went boosting downtown manhattan, on 34 street. He did not make ten cent. I was the one who made the money that day after I sold all my merchandise here he go what I getting. I said what you mean what are you getting. So I told him I guess you ain't really getting nothing from me. Cause if the shoe was on the other foot. And I did not get nothing, and I asked him what am I getting. He would look at me like I'm crazy so all I gave him that day was 50.00. I think I made 200.00 that day. So he go after I handed him 50.00 he didn't say nothing while he was spending it. As soon as he cracked it all up in an hour. Here he comes asking for more money I told him know I had things to do with my money he said like what. First off, I need food to hold me until I get my food stamps he wasn't trying to hear nothing. So I just walked out my apartment here he comes behind me talking about can I get 20.00 more. I told him know so I'm in the supermarket going through the aisles talking about I putting some food in my apartment. I do not smoke crack no more thanks to him cause me and him use to get high together. Go boosting. But one day in 1999. Something came to my head and said bitch you are killing yourself. So one day in 1999. I got up one morning and said fuck the crack and I just started eating regularly. Gaining my weight back he was hating who cares. But I was still boosting drug free cause I was on PA my check every two weeks was 46.00 every two weeks. How could I live off of 46.00 every two weeks. I had a cable bill to pay. So I would go boosting to pay my cable bill. Cause welfare was paying my rent and coned. I was on section-8 got my section-8 in 99. And lost it in 2011. So he would smoke crack all through my apartment. Trying to get me to smoke. I don't think so. So every time he would come in and try and light up. I would do nothing he don't like. Like turning up the radio or start running the water. Are go through my closet are call his moms he be like don't call my mother. While I'm smoking she knew her son was a crackhead. Well for the record I stopped smoking in 1999. And I still ain't smoking so do the math from 99 until 2012. Still ain't smoking nothing can make me go back to using drugs nothing. Not even my miserable mother. She is a miserable person this manspit food in my face. He was just like Raihem a real creep. Now mine you him and Raihem was the same height. But Raihem penis is bigger than his when his shit ain't hard now my ex-husband he wore a size 10 and he did not have a big penis like Raihem what's up with that. Now this other creep I'm going to talk about this other man I was dealing with in 1996 his name was bonnie. I got 12 stiches in my left shoulder from this alcoholic. He was a real alcoholic in 1996. At that time I was in my late 30's he was 52 yrs old. I wish I never met his ass. He was very abusive to me. Me and him went to the hotel on Webster Ave. A couple of times and every time we went to the hotel. I really didn't want to go with him cause I know once we get in the hotel room we would start arguing. He would call me all kinds of names that's when I was smoking crack. He would always by them dollar Bacardi's light. And drink midnight dragon beer and would start on about my drug addiction. I wasn't try to hear that at the time from his drunken ass. Niger look at you you are a fuckin alcoholic. Look who's talking. Anyway a lot of times when he did when he did not have money for me and him to go to Webster Hotel. I would go to sleep with this man on rooftops. But I rob him a couple of times when he would fall asleep in the hotel are on rooftops. Cause he always had a few dollars in his pocket claiming he did not have enough money for us to go to the hotel yeah right. As soon as he go into his drunk sleep. I would wait around 10 min and start searching his pockets. I would find his stash but he claims as he did not have no money all that wore was leather. Only leather. He had every color of leather pants jackets hat. So I mess up a lot of his leather pants by cutting the pocket off to get the wallet. And he use to hide money. In the cuff of his leather pants and I gotta wear his mark on my left arm for the rest of my life. One day he choked me out where as I had to be rushed to Lincoln Hospital. And mind you this incident happened in the park around 3:00 am in the morning. I thought it was just me and him in the part but it wasn't cause there was a man on another bench. Who was an undercover cop. He seen what that bastard was doing to me he ran over threw Bonnie to the ground hand cuffed his ass. Bonnie told the undercover I was trying to rob him. He's telling the cop. I got his walled he kept saying she on drugs and I said he's an alcoholic. He only had 90.00 in his wallet. So I told the officer he got his wallet so the officer checked his pockets and said he is your wallet and the office opened his walled and said there is no money. He go bonnie got it. The cop said miss you need to meet me at the pricent. So you can file a complaint on him. And that's what I did. After that I left that sorry ass alone. He would still come around messing with me trying to buy me. he was kluting for punishment. What an asshole. Men nowadays ain't got respect for women. All they wanna do is use and abuse us. They wanna move in lay up on us cheat on us and they will cheat with your so called girlfriends. Men are pussys most of them not all of them. You still got good men out there somewhere I guess. When a man put his hands on a women he's a real bitch. Cause real man ain't gonna beat on his wife, girlfriend or his mother. I do not want no relationship with a man for awhile cause some men are full of shit and some men are fagets on the downlow. Cause getting back to Raihem when I use to visit his punk ass in the upstate jails. He would sometimes come on the visit teling me Wanda look he's gay. He fucking another man behind the wall. But them fagets will come on the visit and sit and talk to there wife are girlfriend whoever come visit them. Wanna stick their nasty ass tong all down their throat. Knowing he just threw eating ass are getting fucked in the ass. My raihem got raped in jail at 16 yrs.old. now he is 49 years old. I really truly believe he is still seeing other men behind my back. He likes look at rated X movies so when he sees the pussys and dicks I'm asking him what are you looking at the pussys or dick. Cause he would keep rewinding to look at the same part over and over. Then he would catch an attitude saying Wanda please yeah right. You really looking at them big black dicks niger. And he got a lot of gay friends. You seen that movie cover. Remember when Leon play the part liking men. Well I seen cover a couple of times cause got the DVD so when Raihem watched it for the first time he act like he did not want to see Leon play that part. With the man in the shower with him here go raihem I never wanna see that movie again. Yeah right. I came home a few times and caught him watching it. I do not understand why men like men and women like women. God do not appreciate that at all. See I do not wanna be birthed with Raihem no more. He can go about his business when he get out of jail in 2 weeks. He's not gonna last out there. Cause he like smoking crack sniffing dope. He will get violated before Dec. 2012 pullin. Mark my words Raihem 26 yr old son knows what his father did to me over the years. This man use me up like a piece of garbage. But it's okay cause I will always walk with my head in the air. God will make a way for me and mines. I got 2 handsome sons and 4 beautiful granddaughter. When God bless me with a man. I will know I just hope it ain't too late. Cause shit I'm already 49 yrs old. If God let me live to see my 50th birthday. I'm going to do my stand-up mic. I not scare of know audience scare money don't get none I got all of Tyler Perry movies and sometime. His movies make me cry. But all his movies are good for abuse women to watch. Tyler Perry makes me stronger cause I'm not putting up a man bullshit no more. Fuck them. I'm fuck them like they fucked me for yrs. Watch them I get my microphone ain't no stopping me but God look for me on Facebook 2013.

Well this is the End of my Story.

There's more to tell

Aries

Vs.

Aries

This book is for all women all over the world

All sisters all colors all shades

More to be revealed